Warrior Women in American History

I0884135

THE ROLE OF WOMEN IN THE VIETNAM WAR

Warrior Women in American History

THE ROLE OF WOMEN IN THE VIETNAM WAR

Cavendish Square
New York

Hallie Murray

Published in 2020 by Cavendish Square Publishing, LLC

243 5th Avenue, Suite 136, New York, NY 10016

First Edition

Website: cavendishsq.com

Cataloging-in-Publication Data
Names: Murray, Hallie.
Title: The role of women in the Vietnam War / Hallie Murray.
Description: New York : Cavendish Square Publishing, 2020. | Series: Warrior women in American history | Includes glossary and index.
Identifiers: ISBN 9781978514256 (pbk.) | ISBN 9781978514263 (library bound) | ISBN 9781978514270 (ebook)
Subjects: LCSH: United States. Army Nurse Corps–Biography–Juvenile literature. | United States. Army Nurse Corps–Biography–Juvenile literature. | Vietnam War, 1961-1975–Medical care–Juvenile literature. | Vietnam War, 1961-1975–Women--United States–Juvenile literature. | United States–Armed Forces–Nurses–Biography--Juvenile literature.
Classification: LCC DS559.44 M87 2020 | DDC 959.704'37 B–dc23

Printed in the United States of America

Portions of this book originally appeared in *American Women of the Vietnam War* by Amanda Ferguson.

Photo Credits: Cover, p. 3 Everett Collection/Newscom; p. 7 Keystone-France/Gamma-Keystone/Getty Images; pp. 9, 18, 28, 47, 74-75, 84-85 © AP Images; pp. 12-13, 26-27, 66-67, 82-83 Bettmann/Getty Images; p. 20 J. R. Eyerman/The LIFE Picture Collection/Getty Images; p. 23 Heritage Images/Hulton Archive/Getty Images; p. 32 Arnold Sachs/Archive Photos/Getty Images; pp. 34-35 Hulton Archive/Getty Images; pp. 38-39 Sovfoto/Universal Images Group/Getty Images; pp. 40-41 Robert Altman/Archive Photos/Getty Images; p. 45 Everett Historical/Shutterstock.com; p. 51 Women Veterans Health Care/U.S. Department of Veterans Affairs; p. 52 Cvandyke/Shutterstock.com; p. 56 PJF Military Collection/Alamy Stock Photo; pp. 58-59 AFP/Getty Images; p. 61 Everett Collection Inc/Alamy Stock Photo; pp. 62-63 Wally McNamee/Corbis Historical/Getty Images; p. 71 RBM Vintage Images/Alamy Stock Photo; p. 76 MPI/Archive Photos/Getty Images; p. 79 Photo 12/Alamy Stock Photo; p. 87 RGR Collection/Alamy Stock Photo.

Contents

Introduction

In the mid-nineteenth century, the country we know as Vietnam became a French colony. A century later, during World War II, it came under Japanese occupation after France fell to Nazi Germany and its allies. After World War II ended, Japan was forced to leave the country, and Vietnam was officially declared independent and renamed the "Democratic Republic of Vietnam" by its leader, Ho Chi Minh, on September 2, 1945. This wouldn't last, however. France wanted badly to take back its former colony.

At first, the United States was in favor of Vietnam's independence, but the American government knew that Ho Chi Minh was a communist, and fear of communism was rapidly growing. The US government believed that if Ho Chi Minh turned Vietnam into a communist nation, other Southeast Asian countries would follow suit. If communism spread, then capitalist counties like America would lose trade partners and suffer major economic consequences. In order to limit Ho Chi Minh's power, the United States began to fund France's efforts to fight Ho Chi Minh's army and regain control of Vietnam.

Despite this support, France was ultimately unsuccessful, pulling out of the country and the conflict in 1954. The United States worked instead to divide Vietnam politically,

Born in Vietnam around 1890, Ho Chi Minh first became involved in politics while living in France in the 1920s. After Vietnam gained independence from France, he was elected president of the country.

wherein Ho Chi Minh would govern North Vietnam, and Ngo Dinh Diem, an anti-communist, would govern South Vietnam until elections could be held in 1956 regarding reuniting the country under one of the two regimes. But it soon became clear that the Vietnamese people would largely vote for Ho Chi Minh, rather than the Americans' preferred choice of Ngo Dinh Diem. So, with US government support, Ngo Dinh Diem cancelled the election.

Robbed of their democractic power, many Vietnamese citizens were upset, especially those who supported the communist cause. Communist sympathizers in Vietnam joined together into a large political organization called the Vietcong and raised a large guerrilla army in order to overthrow the South Vietnamese government. The United States began to send soldiers and other military personnel into Vietnam to support South Vietnam and Ngo Dinh Diem, and by 1965, America had officially declared war on North Vietnam.

By 1969, more than half a million US troops were stationed in Vietnam, and many more military personnel, including nurses and other roles usually filled by women, had been flown in to engage in the conflict. The US Department of Defense kept no official records specifying the number of women who served in Vietnam, but most sources estimate that between 1962 and 1973, seven thousand to twelve thousand women were assigned to active military duty in the country. The vast majority of these women served as nurses, and all were volunteers.

Although women were not allowed to participate in combat for the first two centuries of America's existence as a country, women have always played a role in the

American president Dwight Eisenhower (*left*) shakes hands with Ngo Dinh Diem, the president of South Vietnam (*right*), in May 1957. Secretary of State John Dulles stands in the center.

United States' military history. While some women did disguise themselves as men in order to fight on the front lines, many countless others engaged in wartime activities at home and behind the scenes, especially in espionage and nursing roles. Some of the most famous spies of the Civil War, including Belle Boyd and Rose Greenhow, were women; in World War I and II, thousands of women held noncombat positions such as mechanics, spies, telephone operators, test pilots, clerks, and nurses. In theory, this allowed men who traditionally held these posts to serve on the battlefield.

By the time of the Vietnam War, women had been much more fully integrated into the military, though they still weren't allowed to engage in combat. Programs that were set up during World War II, like the Women's Army Corps, welcomed volunteers. Many people in America were against the war in Vietnam, but that didn't negate the fact that serving in the military could offer good opportunities for women that weren't necessarily available in civilian jobs.

In the late 1960s, professional opportunities for women in the United States were largely limited to teaching and nursing jobs. Some women viewed serving in Vietnam as an adventure, while others felt obligated to do so out of a sense of duty to their country. Still more were tempted by the military's offer to pay for their education.

Most nurses served a standard one-year tour of duty, and most of these women were in the country between 1969 and 1971, at the time when the greatest number of US troops were stationed in Vietnam. Nurses worked in facilities at all different stages of the conflict—some worked in field hospitals, near the front lines, while others served in surgical facilities or triage units. The few women who weren't nurses worked as military intelligence officers, translators, clerks, and flight controllers. In addition to those who served in the military, more than twenty thousand civilian women, including journalists, teachers, and humanitarians, served in Vietnam with organizations such as USAID and the Red Cross.

In fact, a numbers of women reporters and photographers played a major role in the coverage of the war in Vietnam. Most worked freelance, without the security or benefit of working for a newspaper or television network. Dickey Chapelle, an experienced war photographer who contributed to *Life*, *Reader's Digest*, and *National Geographic*, began covering the war in Vietnam in 1961. She died on November 4, 1965, when a land mine exploded while she was on patrol with a group of marines.

Marguerite Higgins, a journalist who contributed to *Newsday* and the *New York Herald Tribune*, made several trips to Vietnam, beginning in 1963. On her tenth trip to Vietnam in 1965, she contracted a tropical disease and passed away shortly afterward. Other notable female journalists include *New York Times* correspondent Gloria Emerson, who won the George Polk Award for Excellence in Foreign Reporting in 1971, and war correspondent Martha Gellhorn, whose reports were so graphic they were sometimes rejected by her editors.

Though women were not officially allowed to serve on the front lines of combat zones in Vietnam, and would not officially be allowed in combat in the US military until 2013, they often found themselves in combat zones anyway.

Journalist Marguerite Higgins (*right*) talks with Captain Howard Connelly (*left*) in Korea. Higgins worked as a war correspondent during World War II, the Korean War, and the Vietnam War.

Combat zones are often defined by politics rather than actual battle lines. For instance, during the early years of the Vietnam War, men were denied combat pay and compensation because the US government did not want to admit to the public that the military was engaged in combat. Similarly, because few wanted to acknowledge that women were in the line of fire, actual combat zones were not always designated as such.

In the late 1960s and early 1970s, public distrust in the American government and opposition to the war reached an all-time high. In November 1969, the press reported on the investigations of US military atrocities in My Lai. According to reports, a company of US troops entered a Vietnamese village and raped and executed hundreds of unarmed Vietnamese women, children, and men.

In 1971, classified government documents were leaked to the *New York Times*. Known as the Pentagon Papers, the documents revealed that the US government kept many secrets about its involvement in the Vietnam War. Although the US government took the *New York Times* to court, claiming that the paper had no right to publish the leaked information, the Supreme Court ruled in favor of the *Times*, citing the protected constitutional right to freedom of the press.

After the publication of the Pentagon Papers, public opinion of the war and the government fell even more, and soon America pulled out of the war. The last US troops left Vietnam in 1972. The United States had not achieved its political objectives, and the war was considered a North Vietnamese victory. Many Americans viewed the war as a complete and unnecessary waste. With little public or government support, Vietnam veterans were left to deal with the physical, emotional, and social consequences of their service.

The biographies presented here are not intended to represent the Vietnam War experience. Rather, six women explain what the Vietnam War was like for them personally: why they chose to go to Vietnam, what they experienced there, and how those experiences affected them. Like their male counterparts, women who served in Vietnam faced unimaginable physical and mental circumstances. Likewise, when they returned home, they found that few wanted to hear about their experiences. Today, trauma and the psychological effects of being in a war zone are better understood, but veterans still don't always receive the support they need. Attempting to understand the experiences of individuals who witnessed the war firsthand can help us both better grasp the war as a historical event and empathize in some way with those who served.

1

Treatment for All: Army Nurse Kathy Fennel

As a young woman, Kathy Fennel was inspired by the work of Dr. Tom Dooley, a physician who volunteered with refugee camps and established clinics throughout Southeast Asia. The hospitals Dooley was associated with treated more than half a million people for illnesses such as smallpox, leprosy, malnutrition, and malaria, and Dooley wrote several books about his experiences, many of which significantly influenced public opinion of Vietnam.

Dooley passed away in 1961, but Fennel was greatly affected by his accounts of his work and wanted to bring the same aid to Southeast Asian citizens. While in nursing school, Fennel realized that if she wanted to be a nurse in Vietnam, it would likely have to be done for the military. She enlisted after graduating and secured an assignment in an operating room due to her experience in the area.

On the Ground in Vietnam

Fennel arrived in Vietnam shortly after the Tet Offensive. Tet is the Vietnamese New Year, based on the lunar calendar. Traditionally, military forces recognized a truce over Tet. The Vietnamese spend the holiday tending graves and paying tribute to their ancestors. On the eve of Tet

Tom Dooley

Thomas Anthony Dooley III was born on January 17, 1927, in St. Louis, Missouri. He served in a naval hospital in the mid-1940s and reenlisted after getting his medical degree in 1953. A year later, Dooley was recruited by the CIA to collect medical information from Vietnamese citizens and to serve as the face of American humanitarian action in Southeast Asia. Dooley worked in refugee camps and was encouraged to write about his experiences. His book, *Deliver Us from Evil*, became a best seller when it was published in 1956 and chronicled his humanitarian work as well as the horrors committed by the communist regime in Vietnam. However, in the late 1990s it was revealed that much of what Dooley had written was exaggerated and occasionally completely false. Dooley's work has been cited as a major influence on public opinion of early US involvement in Vietnam. Dooley died of cancer in 1961 at just thirty-four.

in 1968, however, the Vietcong launched a major attack against US and South Vietnamese forces in more than one hundred towns and cities. The Vietcong even attacked the US Embassy in Saigon, killing five marines.

Although the offensive was technically a defeat for the Vietcong—37,000 Vietcong soldiers were killed, compared to 2,500 American casualties, and US troops overtook every city that had been captured—it proved that the US government and military had miscalculated the Vietcong's strength and ability. The Tet Offensive shook the confidence of the American public, which had been told that a US victory was close at hand.

Dr. Tom Dooley poses with patients at a Medical International Co-Operation (MEDICO) hospital in Muong Sing, Laos, in 1959.

Fennel was assigned to work at the Twelfth Evacuation Hospital in Cu Chi, a province about 30 miles (48 kilometers) northwest of Saigon. Sandwiched between Saigon and the Cambodian border, the hospital was in an area where heavy fighting happened. Most of the buildings on the hospital compound were Quonset huts that did little to keep out the heavy rains during monsoon (the rainy) season. During the dry season, the wind blew sand everywhere, making it difficult to keep wounds clean. When Fennel wasn't on duty, she spent time in her hooch (tent), reading, listening to music, and catching up on sleep.

After her first month in Vietnam, the twenty-three-year-old began to question the US government's honesty about the war. The numbers of officially reported casualties did not match what she was seeing. "And we were only one small hospital," she notes. "It seemed to me that we weren't winning, that something was wrong. I didn't know what that was, but you couldn't look at that kind of trauma and still believe it made sense."[1]

Caring for the Enemy

Fennel had little time to resolve these questions; she had too many patients to care for, both American and Vietnamese. Under the principles of the Geneva Conventions and the Hippocratic oath, all patients had to receive humane medical treatment. This included prisoners of war, of course. This proved difficult for some American medical staff and wounded GIs, or members of the armed forces. Sometimes staff and wounded Americans directed their anger and frustration over the war toward Vietnamese patients.

This aerial view shows Quonset huts used for storage and housing. Quonset huts are lightweight steel structures that were used primarily by the United States in World War II and in Vietnam.

"There were times that I had resentments," Fennel admits. "I'd think, 'I'm tired; I don't want to get up and take care of Vietnamese patients, because in a few hours I have to do it again for Americans.' We all had those feelings, but we were young and exhausted. We didn't understand."[2] The close proximity of Vietnamese and American wounded sometimes had more positive effects; recuperating patients sometimes gained respect and compassion for each other as fellow soldiers who suffered similar injuries.

Shortages of equipment and staff—and the severity of conditions—forced the hospital staff to be creative. Fennel notes that the hard work and experimental surgery and treatment done in Vietnam later led to important medical advances. In particular, many important advances in artery and blood vessel work were made thanks to the efforts of military doctors and nurses to save the limbs of wounded soldiers.

Going Above and Beyond

In addition to medical work, nurses provided solace and spiritual comfort. Patients often turned to nurses for a final moment of emotional contact. To them, nurses represented the mothers, girlfriends, or wives they would never see again. Although it was difficult to cope with such moments, nurses understood how vital it was that patients not die alone.

Fennel is haunted by the memory of a young GI who had been in a mine accident. Shot through his stomach, the man's entire buttocks had been blown away; he was dying. "He grabbed my hand and wouldn't let go," she remembers. "He was married, a young kid. He was like Godzilla, he was so strong. I tried to pry his fingers off

The Hippocratic Oath

The Hippocratic oath is an ancient oath traditionally taken by physicians. It is named after Hippocrates, a Greek physician known as the "Father of Medicine" and who is often considered the first person to understand that diseases were caused by things in nature rather than by gods or supernatural forces. The earliest examples of the Hippocratic oath are from Greek fragments dating to around 275 BCE. Today, the Hippocratic oath has been replaced by more official legal documents regarding medical ethics, but people still refer to the Hippocratic oath and use it as shorthand for the ethical obligations of medical professionals. For instance, the well-known idea that doctors must "first do no harm"—meaning that doctors are ethically forbidden from doing anything that will cause harm—comes from the Hippocratic oath.

because his wedding ring was hurting my hand. He turned to me and screamed 'Henrietta!' At that moment, I was as good as Henrietta. He knew he was dying. I could feel him totally relaxing as if he were melting. He was pronounced dead. They took off the tubes, and I was left to get him off the table. We had thirty more patients to deal with. I couldn't believe that I was talking to this kid and he was alive and strong, even though he was bleeding out everywhere. And then he was dead."[3]

Sometimes, nurses were left to deal with emotionally charged situations because no one else would. Fennel remembers once when a US helicopter pilot asked the hospital to tend to a young Vietnamese woman. In order to get the hospital to admit her, he said that the woman

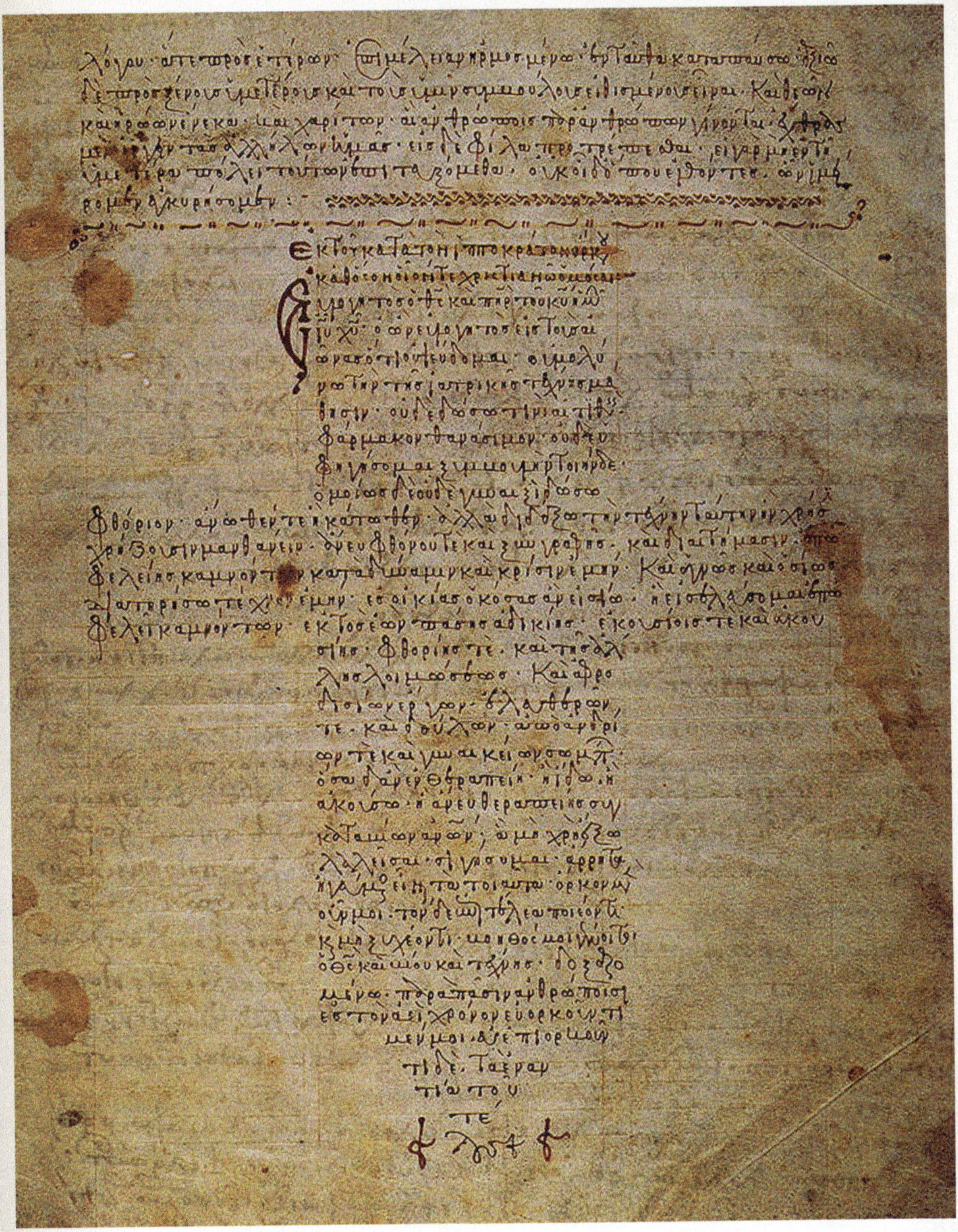

This artifact from the collection of the Vatican Apostolic Library shows a copy of the Hippocratic oath found in a Byzantine manuscript from the 1100s.

had been shot in the stomach. As it turned out, the woman wasn't wounded; she was in labor, three months before the baby was due. A doctor on staff specialized in delivering babies back in the States. He wasn't willing to get out of bed to help in the delivery. He wanted to preserve his strength for the next round of incoming wounded soldiers.

Fennel was ordered to deliver the baby. The situation was hopeless. Without the advanced medical technology and equipment that is available today, premature babies had little chance of survival, even in ideal conditions. Fennel was ordered to help the woman as best she could. "What I was seeing was the terminal moment," she says. "All the men had left. Nobody wanted to deal with it. Eventually, it's always the patient and the nurse. I remember seeing the baby's corpse in the basin and thinking, this shouldn't be happening."[4] The event came to symbolize the war for Fennel; the images from that day continue to haunt her.

Returning to the United States

The daily grind was depressing. Fennel coped with her depression by spending time with friends. Although she was a ranking officer, the hospital staff generally ignored rules forbidding fraternization between officers and non-ranking military. "We got yelled at for doing it, but the people who worked in the operation room [OR] would do things together, even if it was just sit in the OR and talk. If you were down, they helped you get back up; if they were down, you helped them. It was the only way to stay sane."[5]

Fennel left Vietnam a few months earlier than she had intended. A swimming accident left her with a serious neck injury. She was sent to the United States on medical evacuation. She spent the remainder of her service recuperating at the Valley Forge General Hospital in Pennsylvania. Gradually, she switched from recovering patient to part-time operating nurse. She was discharged from the Army Nurse Corps in 1969.

In 1971, she married another Vietnam veteran, a former army medic. Over the next decade, the couple began raising a family. She worried about the chances of her children developing health problems as a result of the Agent Orange she'd been exposed to in Vietnam. From 1961 to 1971, the US Air Force sprayed millions of gallons of the highly toxic chemical in order to destroy forests where Vietcong (VC) troops might be hiding, as well as to destroy crops that might be providing the VC army with food. Agent Orange has since been identified as the cause of many serious health problems, including cancer, diabetes, and birth defects.

Fennel also made sure she was tested for hepatitis C, a blood-borne disease she risked contracting, because in Vietnam her hands were immersed in blood without rubber gloves. Eventually, she returned to school to become a physician's aide, a job that allows her to work closely with doctors.

Operation Smile

In 1993, Fennel and her husband returned to Vietnam with Operation Smile, a volunteer organization group that funds and coordinates cleft lip and palate surgery in developing countries. During her flight to Da Nang, she read a biography about Sharon Ann Lane, a nurse who was killed during a mortar attack on the 312th Evacuation Hospital in Chu Lai. She was touched by the fact that

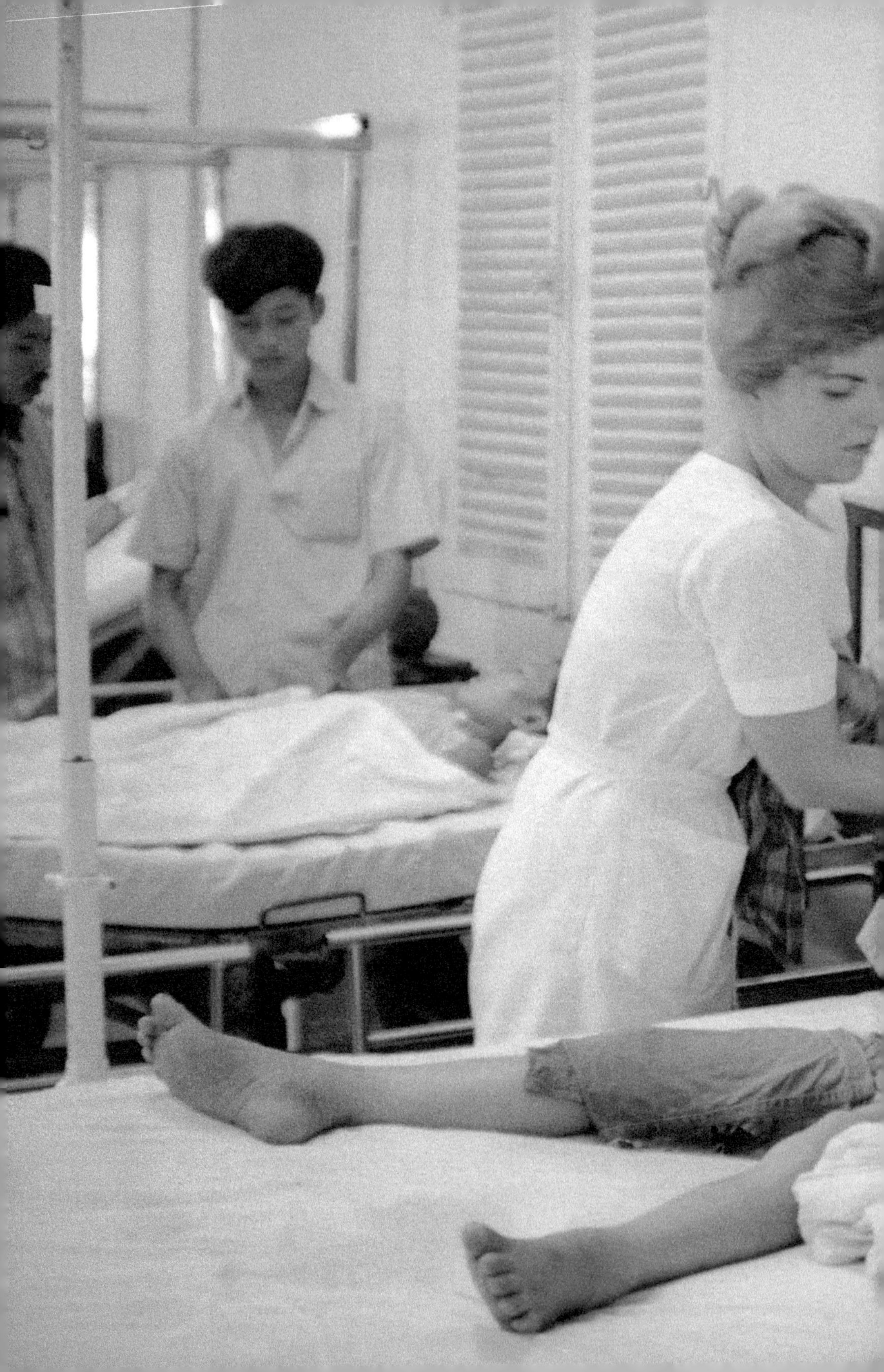

Combat nurses in Vietnam often treated civilians, including women and children, as well as soldiers. In this 1966 image, Nurse Karen Walters takes a wounded baby from its mother for care.

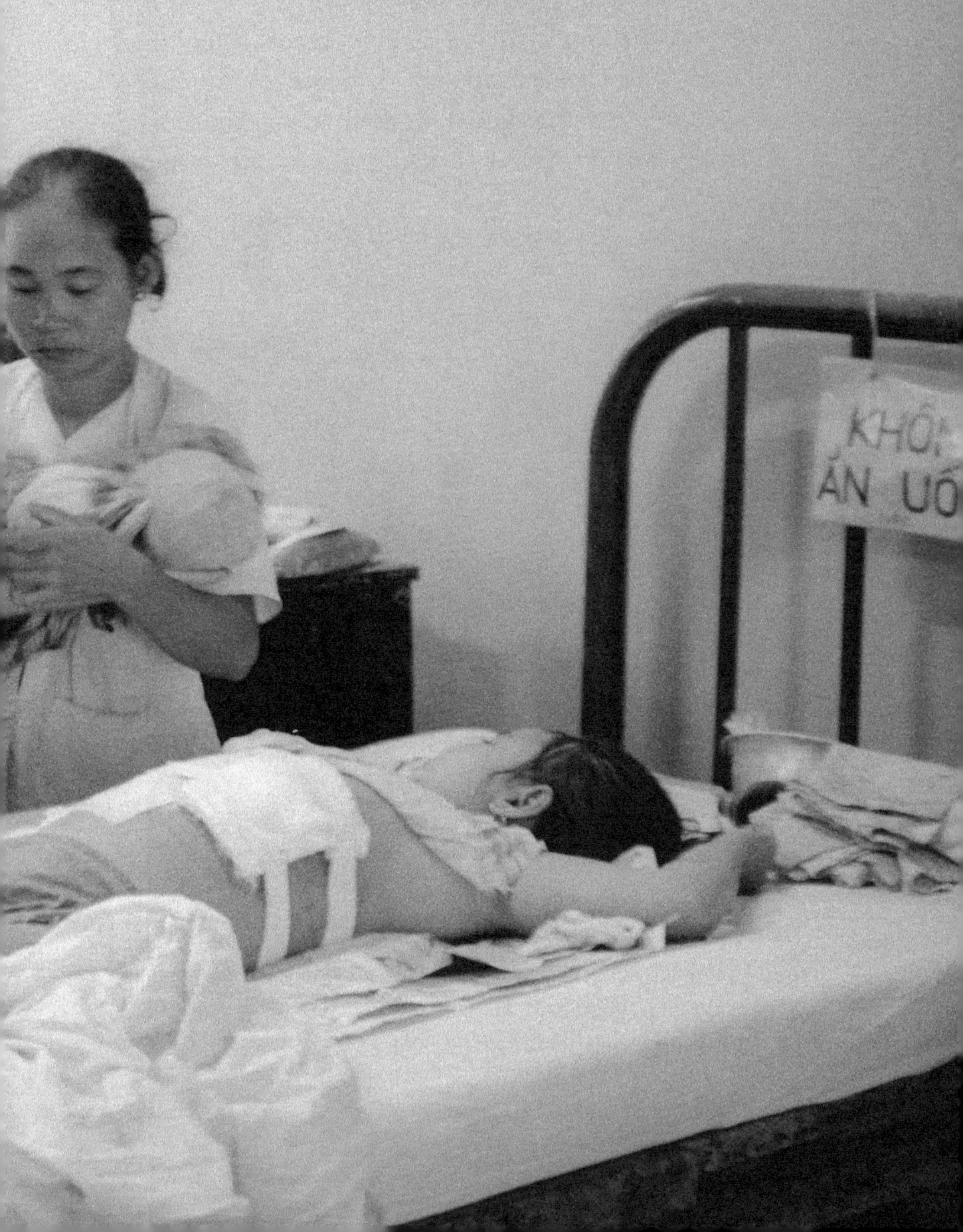

Lane had volunteered to work in the Vietnamese ward. It was an assignment that most nurses took with reluctance. Lane worked hard to treat her patients with compassion, no matter what side they were fighting on.

With the blessing of Lane's mother, Fennel established the Sharon Ann Lane Foundation in honor of the young nurse's legacy. The foundation worked to build and fund a medical clinic in Chu Lai, dedicated to the memory

A military officer congratulates Nurse Sharon Ann Lane during her promotion to first lieutenant in 1968. Lane passed away in 1969 when she was hit by hostile fire in Vietnam.

of Sharon Ann Lane and the children of Vietnam. The foundation also worked with the Hue Medical School in Hue, Vietnam's former imperial capital, to establish a medical educational exchange program. Fennel returned to Vietnam from time to time to help with the program.

Fennel's work with the clinic helped her come to terms with her former experiences in Vietnam. "I didn't have a lot of time to play with Vietnamese children during the war," she explains. "I do now. There is a beauty in what's happening here. Now we're involved with working towards a present and a future."[6]

2

Building and Rebuilding: USAID Administrator Barbara Rozell

Though she was the daughter of an army colonel, Barbara Rozell was deeply uncomfortable with the Vietnam War. Graphic images of the war appeared on the evening news, and when Rozell became involved in San Francisco's counterculture movement in the 1960s, she found that many of her friends were extremely against American involvement in the conflict. Her family, on the other hand, was strongly supportive of the military. "It was so big at the universities to be antiwar, antigovernment, burn the flag," she says. "That just went against my core values as the daughter of a military officer whose way of life had always been country first, family second, and yourself third. I had this need to go over and figure out for myself whether or not we should be there."[1]

When Rozell saw an ad in the paper announcing that the United States Agency for International Development (USAID) was seeking administrative staff to work in Vietnam, she realized this might be her opportunity to find

USAID

The United States Agency for International Development is an aid organization that was established by President John F. Kennedy in 1961 following the passage of the Foreign Assistance Act, which reorganized certain foreign aid programs of the US government. USAID is an independent agency, but its missions are largely informed by US foreign policy and the direction of the National Security Council, including the president. During the Vietnam War, under President Richard Nixon, the Foreign Assistance Act was revised to prioritize "Basic Human Needs," including food, health, and education, rather than economic aid. Today, there are USAID missions in over one hundred countries globally.

out for herself whether the war in Vietnam seemed justified. The agency was an independent government agency under the US State Department. Its duties were to coordinate humanitarian relief projects, such as building schools, sending teachers and doctors to villages, and sending agricultural specialists to help replant crops destroyed in war. Working for USAID seemed to Rozell like a good way to both serve the US government and work toward principles of peace.

Civilian Volunteers

In addition to those enlisted in the military, thousands of civilian women volunteered to go to Vietnam to support the troops, the US government, and the Vietnamese civilian population. Some were foreign service employees and worked for the CIA, the US Embassy, and with USAID.

President John F. Kennedy appears at a press conference circa 1963. Kennedy served as United States president from 1961 to his death in 1963 and established USAID by executive order in 1961.

Others were part of the military civilian workforce, working for the Armed Forces Radio and Television, the Military Assistance Command Vietnam, or the Army Special Services.

The Red Cross Supplemental Recreational Activities Overseas program sent women ages twenty-one to twenty-five to Vietnam to boost the morale of American troops. Nicknamed "donut dollies," the women ran recreation centers throughout Vietnam. They also went out to remote areas in the mountains and jungles to entertain the troops. Because the roads were dangerous, they were usually transported by helicopter. They invented their own programs, lugging canvas bags filled with homemade games and prizes out with them to the fields. Although the games were silly, most men welcomed the distraction and the company.

The United Service Organization (USO), founded by various religious groups, also ran recreation clubs for soldiers. The USO recruited women to work as hostesses at the centers, where soldiers could eat, play cards and Ping-Pong, get free haircuts, make overseas calls, or see a concert. At the USO center in Tan Son Nhut, volunteer Maureen Nerli recalls, "We served between five hundred and eight hundred shakes, hot dogs, and hamburgers every day."[2]

Other organizations focused on aiding Vietnamese civilians. The American Friends Service Committee, a Quaker organization, worked to bring medical assistance to war victims. In the Peace Corps and the International Volunteer Service, women helped build schools, run health clinics and orphanages, and provide other humanitarian assistance.

Stopover in Hong Kong

It took six months for Rozell to process the necessary paperwork and security clearances. In January 1968, she went to Washington, DC, for a month of orientation. Her orientation included a brief introduction to Vietnamese culture, language, and economics. She also received an overview of the agency's mission. Shortly afterward, she was on her way to Vietnam.

The flight to Saigon was long. Rozell and two other USAID colleagues decided to stop in Hong Kong for the night. They wanted to be fresh when they arrived in Saigon. The next morning, they waited to board their flight. Hours went by. What was the holdup? Rumors flew: an enormous VC offensive had taken place; the VC had taken over Saigon; the VC had taken over all airports. As it turns out, the women had arrived in the middle of the Tet Offensive.

With no money, work, or official orders, Rozell began her war experience stuck in Hong Kong until further notice. She contacted the US consulate in Hong Kong for advice. They told her that the

Comedian Bob Hope performs at a 1967 USO show meant to entertain troops and maintain morale in Vietnam. Hope was deeply involved in the USO and in supporting American troops.

only thing they could do to help was to bail her out of jail in case the manager of her hotel decided to arrest her for not being able to pay her hotel bill. After several days of waiting for further instruction, a US officer told her that there would be a military flight to Saigon the next morning; if there were any empty seats available, there was a possibility that they would take civilians. The same afternoon, word came from Washington, DC, that the situation in Vietnam was very dangerous. If she wanted, the agency would assign her to a different post. Despite the risks involved, Barbara decided to go to Saigon. "I don't think I was scared," she says. "At twenty-two, you feel infallible."[3]

The Tet Offensive was still going on when she arrived in Saigon. Curfews were in effect, and the threat of terrorism was high. Vietnamese civilians were not allowed to go to their jobs at US government agencies. Gradually, curfews eased and Vietnamese employees were allowed to return to work.

Public Works, Private Aims

Rozell worked for a USAID program division manager. USAID aimed to earn the trust and loyalty of the Vietnamese population through public works programs. USAID field workers performed such tasks as setting up water systems, schools, and health clinics, and bringing electricity to small villages. They were required to send progress reports to USAID program officers in Saigon. The program officers coordinated the field workers' activities, estimated program costs, and prepared budget reports that would be put before Congress for approval in the national budget. Rozell's job was to help prepare these reports.

Two months into her stay, Rozell began to feel that the goals of the USAID program were at cross-purposes with the military. What good was it for the US government to fund public works projects in local villages when those villages might be bombed by the US military? Who, then, was the enemy? One night, she sat on the roof of her hotel, looking out over the river onto a little jungle area. She remembers:

> I looked up and saw two jets circling on either side. One would swoop down and drop some kind of bomb—you'd see this amazing explosion of light and smoke. As soon as he finished his arc, the one from the other side would come down and do the same thing. At the same time, choppers came in and dropped a bunch of soldiers who ran into the jungle. I could hear the machine gun fire and see little puffs of smoke, maybe from grenades. A little while later, they all came running out of the jungle. Some guys got picked up by gunships. Some guys were on stretchers and got picked up by medical helicopters. Then they were gone. So now did we own the jungle? Did the VC own the jungle? I began to think, you know, this just doesn't feel right. Why are we doing this?[4]

She also became aware that many US civilians and military personnel living in Saigon did not respect the South Vietnamese military, whom they were supposedly supporting. "We called the Vietnamese military White Mice. We didn't have a lot of faith in them," she recalls.[5] She says that curfews set by the South Vietnamese

Vietcong soldiers charge against South Vietnamese government forces during the Tet Offensive in 1968.

government and military were frequently ignored. "I went across a bridge in a Jeep one time with a guy. A South Vietnamese soldier told us to stop. We ignored him and drove right on our merry way," she says.[6]

Difficult Choices

When her eighteen-month assignment in Saigon was over, Rozell decided to leave Vietnam. She felt she had done her job as best she could. Staying would serve no further purpose. "I didn't want to be a war groupie," she says.[7] She considered working for USAID in Turkey. But it occurred to her that she did not want to live in another country where she would be working and living in an isolated American community. "I was having dinner with some of my cohorts, and I started to listen to the conversation around me," she explains. "People were saying, 'I can't find any good servants,' 'We can't get any

Antiwar protesters in San Francisco circa April 1969 hold signs and noisemakers. That month, antiwar parades took place across the country in cities including New York and Washington, DC.

fresh meat at the commissary,' and 'Liquor's really getting expensive.' I'd heard this conversation too many times. I could go to Turkey and hear the same conversation; it wouldn't make any difference what country I was in."[8]

In 1969, Rozell returned to San Francisco. The antiwar movement had now turned explosive. She became guarded when talking about her experiences in Vietnam and eventually avoided the subject altogether. "If you even mentioned the word 'Vietnam', you had no idea what kind of response you were going to get. My stomach would turn in knots. I knew that people would discount what I had done or would turn and literally walk away. They didn't want to hear about personal experiences; it was too raw."[9]

Life After the War

While in San Francisco, Rozell reconnected with a former boyfriend. They soon married. When the couple began raising a family, she didn't work much outside of the home. She sometimes wonders what life would have been like if she'd continued working for the State Department. Ultimately, though, she's happy with the life and the adventures she's had with her family.

In 1995, Rozell decided to go on a tour of Vietnam with a group of women who had served there in various capacities. Connie Stevens, a performer who entertained US troops in Vietnam 1969 and 1970, filmed the trip for a documentary, *A Healing*. The chance to talk with others who had had similar experiences helped put Rozell's time in Vietnam into perspective. She has since shown the film at several schools, using it as a springboard to talk about the Vietnam War. The film has even helped her share her experiences with those closest to her.

She was particularly surprised by her son's rapt interest in the documentary; she had thought that, since he already knew about her service, the three-hour film might be dull for him. Instead, it sharpened his appreciation for what his mother had gone through. "A number of times it brought tears to his eyes," she says. "When it was finished, he said 'Mom, those women were amazing. I would love to meet those women.'"[10]

3

Healing in a War Zone: Army Nurse Diane Carlson Evans

Diane Carlson Evans was born in 1946 and grew up on a dairy farm in Minnesota. Her brother was drafted to fight in 1966, and Evans's parents were relieved when he received orders to go to Korea instead of serving active duty in Vietnam. Little did they know that their daughter would end up serving in Vietnam instead. Evans was not the first woman in her family to serve in the military. Her aunt had risen through the ranks in the Women's Army Corps during World War II and had earned a doctorate degree under the GI Bill (a law giving money to returning members of the military for education). She told Evans that if it hadn't been for the military, she would not have had those opportunities.

Enlisting with the Army Nurse Corps

Evans followed the war in Vietnam with great interest. Her roommate at nursing school had spent a year in Vietnam. She told Evans how desperate the military was to recruit nurses. Evans wanted to practice her nursing skills where

This recruitment poster for the Women's Auxiliary Army Corps (which became the Women's Army Corps in 1943) emphasizes patriotism and encourages women to engage with the war effort.

they were most needed, so she went to an army recruiter to find out how to join. The fact that the Army Nurse Corps would pay for her senior year at nursing school was a benefit. When she told her parents that she had enlisted, they were stunned.

Evans did not tell many of her friends or classmates that she had volunteered to serve in the increasingly unpopular war. Those she did tell questioned her decision. They told her that she didn't seem like the type. At the time, many people assumed that women who joined the military were masculine or unattractive, unable to find a husband and lead a "normal" civilian life.

Undaunted, Evans went to Fort Sam Houston in Texas for six weeks of basic training. She also had some field training at Camp Bullis, where she learned to pitch tents and set up gurneys (wheeled stretchers) and field hospitals. None of this prepared her for what she would face in Vietnam. Looking back, she is resentful that the military did not prepare her for combat: "I think that it was a stereotype: women are the weaker sex so we won't train them; we won't give them weapons to protect themselves with because the men will protect them. Well, if they were going to send us into a combat zone, which they did, we should have been trained to protect ourselves. We should have been able to carry a gun if we needed one. Our training should have been more in depth, and we should have learned how to take care of each other during times of mass casualties and tragedy."[1]

Indescribable Challenges

Evans spent the first half of her tour of duty at the Thirty-Sixth Evacuation Hospital, a surgical and rehabilitation hospital in Vung Tau in South Vietnam. Most of the arriving patients had been treated at other hospitals and came to Vung Tau for delayed surgery. Their wounds had already been cleaned, and they arrived in clean blue pajamas. Evans wanted to go farther north, closer to the fighting and closer to where the wounded were coming in. She requested a transfer and was sent to the Seventy-First Evacuation Hospital at Pleiku, near the Cambodian border.

An army nurse in a hospital at Nha Trang in February 1965 comforts a soldier who was wounded during a Vietcong attack on two US military compounds at Pleiku.

Evans got her wish. The Seventy-First EVAC was in one of the highest combat zones in Vietnam. Helicopters delivered wounded men from fields that were minutes away from the hospital. Sometimes casualties arrived fifty at a time. It was difficult, but necessary, to determine which patients would be treated first—staff and supplies were limited. "That's where a lot of guilt came in," she says. "If we'd only had more supplies, more doctors, more nurses; if this patient wouldn't have had to wait three hours for surgery, maybe he would have survived. Yet we could only do what we could."[2]

Evans wrote home but was unable to describe the reality of her work. Years later, she had a chance to read the letters she'd sent her parents. "When I read those letters, I sat there in shock. If they hadn't been in my own handwriting, I wouldn't have believed I'd written them."[3] Because she hadn't wanted her parents to worry, Evans had written about the weather, friends, and parties—anything besides the war. Every once in a while, though, a detail would slip out. "I would write something like, 'Oh, we were rocketed last night,' but then I'd end everything with, 'Don't worry about me, I'm fine.'"[4] She also had trouble admitting to herself what she was experiencing: "I started a diary in Vietnam and quit writing in it. I decided I didn't want to remember any of this stuff, so why write it down?"[5]

Transitioning into Civilian Life

When her tour of duty ended, Evans returned to Minnesota. She found that many stereotypes about women in the military remained unchanged. On her first day of work at the North Memorial Hospital in Minneapolis, the head nurse was skeptical that Evans had actually served in Vietnam: "First she looked at my feet, and then every inch of me up from there. Finally she sneered, 'You don't look like you've been in the military.' I thought, what am I supposed to look like?"[6]

The routine responsibilities at the civilian hospital were unsatisfying in comparison to the challenges of combat nursing. She had trouble comforting patients who suffered from relatively minor aches and pains. After the challenges and freedoms she'd experienced as a combat nurse, the new bureaucracy and professional protocol she was expected to adhere to felt stifling. She decided to return to the military and was sent to Fort Sam Houston, where she was appointed head nurse in the surgical intensive care unit, treating wounded soldiers returning from combat. "In a way, I was right back in Vietnam," she explains. "I was taking care of the soldiers again, and I was really happy doing that."[7]

In Vietnam, she had never had time to talk to her patients or care for them after their initial treatment. In Texas, she was able to spend time with patients. Working with veterans helped her process her own Vietnam experiences and adjust to civilian life. At the same time, the opportunity to know her patients better was challenging. In Vietnam, she only had time to deal with patients' initial physical injuries. Now, she watched soldiers and their loved ones deal with the longer-term consequences of those injuries: "I had to talk to the families and prepare them for what they were going to see when they went into the intensive care unit, that their son or fiancé had lost both his legs and both his arms in Vietnam. It was very stressful to see how traumatic this was for the families."[8]

PTSD

Post-traumatic stress disorder (PTSD) is a condition that sometimes develops after a person goes through a traumatic event, like war or some kind of assault. Not everyone who goes through trauma develops PTSD. PTSD can present in a lot of different ways, but it is usually characterized by a severe and disruptive stress response that is triggered by benign events and continues to occur over a month after the trauma. PTSD is common among veterans of all ages, though it has historically been misunderstood in many ways. When soldiers returning from World War I exhibited PTSD symptoms, they were diagnosed with "shell shock," and many people believed it was a sign of cowardice. Today, PTSD is better understood by doctors and the public, but we have a long way to go toward fully helping everyone experiencing the condition.

The Vietnam Women's Memorial Project

While working at the Veterans Administration, she met her future husband. In 1972, the couple decided to start a family. When she learned she was pregnant, Evans left the military but continued to nurse part-time. In 1980, with four children to care for, she quit nursing altogether. For many years, she tried to forget her experiences in Vietnam; the memories were too painful. After Evans went to Washington, DC, for the dedication of the Vietnam Veterans Memorial in 1982, she found herself thinking about her time in Vietnam.

She sought out other female veterans and discovered that, like her, many had never talked about their experiences. In 1984, she co-founded the Vietnam

This March 2017 poster from the National Center for PTSD and the women's health initiative of the Veterans Administration encourages female veterans to seek treatment for PTSD.

Women's Memorial Project, which sought to identify and honor civilian and military women who had served in Vietnam and to educate the public about their role in history. The organization was also dedicated to promoting research of service-related health issues, including post-traumatic stress disorder (PTSD) and the effects of Agent Orange.

It took ten years to raise the funding and support to create the memorial, and members of the Vietnam Women's Memorial Project struggled for permission to place the monument on the National Mall in Washington, DC, near the Vietnam Veterans Memorial. In 1988, Evans spoke to a number of national veterans' service organizations and

The Vietnam Women's Memorial in Washington, DC, was dedicated in November 1993 and honors the American women who served in the Vietnam War.

requested their legislative support: "We wish to stand near the Wall of names of those we cared for in death and the bronze statue portraying those we helped come home. We were with them in war and we want to be with them now. I want the women who served to know that they are not forgotten, that there's a special place for them, too, on honored ground."[9]

On November 11, 1993, the Vietnam Women's Memorial was dedicated as part of the Vietnam Veterans Memorial. Located in Washington, DC, a few yards away from the Wall (as the Vietnam Veterans Memorial is called), the memorial features a bronze sculpture by artist Glenna Goodacre of three female Vietnam veterans, one of whom tends a wounded soldier.

4

A Hospital at Sea: Navy Nurse Beth Marie Murphy

After graduating from nursing school, Beth Marie Murphy was assigned to work in a military hospital in the United States. As the situation in Vietnam worsened, more and more troops and other service personnel were needed to keep up the fight. Army and navy recruiters made regular rounds through the hospital asking for volunteers to go to Vietnam.

Murphy didn't know much about what was going on in Vietnam beyond the fact that America was at war, but she'd been inspired by her roommate's father, who was a marine, and decided to enlist, choosing the navy because she'd liked that recruiter best. Murphy would be serving with the Navy Nurse Corps, the nursing arm of the navy's physicians. Murphy's parents weren't pleased when they learned she'd signed up, but she held firm against their objections; she liked the idea of being able to serve her country and travel the world at the same time.

Danger All Around

Murphy had six weeks of naval nursing training at a base in Rhode Island. Training consisted primarily of learning how to march and salute, how to wear a uniform properly, and how to jump off a ship into the ocean. Although she had been told that it was unlikely that she would be sent to Vietnam for at least two years, within three months she received orders to go there. In order not to upset her parents, she didn't tell them she would be serving in Vietnam until the day before she left.

Assigned to work on the USS *Sanctuary*, twenty-two-year-old Murphy figured she would be safe on the ship. When she arrived at the airport in Da Nang, there was no one to meet her or tell her where she was supposed to go. Two men offered to drive her to the US Naval Hospital in Da Nang. There, they told her, she could find transportation to the ship. As they made their way to the hospital, something blew up directly behind their jeep. "All of a sudden, I realized I could really get hurt," she recalls.[1]

Treating Patients on the USS *Sanctuary*

Hovering about 1 mile (1.6 km) off of the Vietnamese coast in the South China Sea, the USS *Sanctuary* was a large multideck hospital with a staff of 750. The boat traveled up and down the Vietnamese coast, servicing the area between Da Nang and the demilitarized zone, where most marines were stationed. Helicopters flew most patients to the ship directly from the battlefield. Occasionally, small Vietnamese boats would deliver sick and injured patients. This turned out to be dangerous, Murphy learned. There was always a chance that a mother begging doctors to take her child aboard might be a Vietcong soldier waiting for a chance to launch a grenade. Despite the risk of terrorism, Murphy remembers that the gangplank was always lowered. As it turns out, US soldiers who forgot to unload their live ammunition before they boarded posed a greater threat to the ship's security.

Without the dirt and dust that plagued most field hospitals, doctors and nurses could perform more

The USS *Sanctuary* was a hospital ship built during World War II and used by the US Navy in World War II and the Vietnam War.

Women Soldiers of the Vietcong

In part to gain popularity, the communist government of North Vietnam focused significantly on increasing gender equality and providing opportunities for women. They created new laws to reduce sexual violence and child marriage and worked to create jobs and other public roles for women. When the war against South Vietnam began, women were major participants in the Vietcong's wartime strategy, including combat. An estimated two hundred thousand highly skilled and trained women served in the North Vietnamese and Vietcong armies. They spied on American and South Vietnamese troops, operated underground communications networks, set traps, smuggled food and weapons, and even commanded soldiers. The efforts of these women contributed significantly to the Vietcong's eventual victory.

complicated surgeries on the ship. The ship had open-heart machines and one of the only two hyperbaric chambers in the country. However, because the boat was in constant motion, the staff had to take precautions to secure the beds and medical equipment. Everything, even bottles, had to be tied down.

An Uphill Battle

Murphy worked on the international ward. Most of her patients were Vietnamese women and children. Confined to the ship, she spent her free time playing with the wounded children. It was emotionally difficult to nurse the children back to health and then send them back to face an uncertain future. She and her colleagues had little say about what happened to their patients. Still, they tried their best to help their patients, even if it meant bending the rules.

Once, a GI brought in a malnourished baby girl that he had found in a garbage can. After the nurses stabilized the girl's condition, they were told that they had to send her to an orphanage. But the nurses couldn't find an orphanage they wanted to send her to. "The officer insisted we discharge her, and so we did," Murphy says. "The same day, we happened to admit a baby boy into the ward; we'd just dressed her up in boy's clothes."[2]

Murphy also worked on the orthopedic and general wards. In the orthopedic ward, many patients suffered the loss of multiple limbs, usually by stepping on land mines or during heavy artillery shelling. On the general ward, patients suffered

A female Vietcong soldier aims an antitank gun during a battle in the Cuu Long delta in South Vietnam. Women held major roles in the Vietcong's war effort, including as soldiers and spies.

from various illnesses, including malaria. Sometimes, she nursed a patient on the general ward back to health, only to receive the same patient on the orthopedic ward days later, now missing his legs or arms. She began to feel run-down, both mentally and physically. She no longer believed the Vietnamese were the enemy. Like others, she questioned the US government's honesty: "The government would report one thing and we'd see something very different. They would say that we were winning the war and suffering very few casualties, and we'd be inundated with casualties."[3]

Overqualified and Unsatisfied

When she returned to the United States, Murphy was not sure what she should do. She decided to remain in the military and was assigned to work at a small naval hospital in California. It was difficult to adapt to her new working environment. "I was used to doing really good nursing," she says. "In Vietnam, we were starting IVs, doing major medical dressing changes, writing medical orders—things we were told in nursing school that we would never do."[4] Protocol did not allow her to practice her medical expertise, and so she decided to return to Vietnam. Knowing that there was demand for flight nurses, she signed up for the Air Force Nurse Corps. However, shortly before she was to begin her assignment, Murphy injured her knee and was disqualified from flight status. Eight months later, she left the military for good.

After her experience at the naval hospital, she had little interest in returning to nursing. "At that time, nurses were basically doctors' handmaids," she explains. Instead, she joined a Catholic convent and tried to put her experiences in Vietnam behind her. "I think I was trying to make life

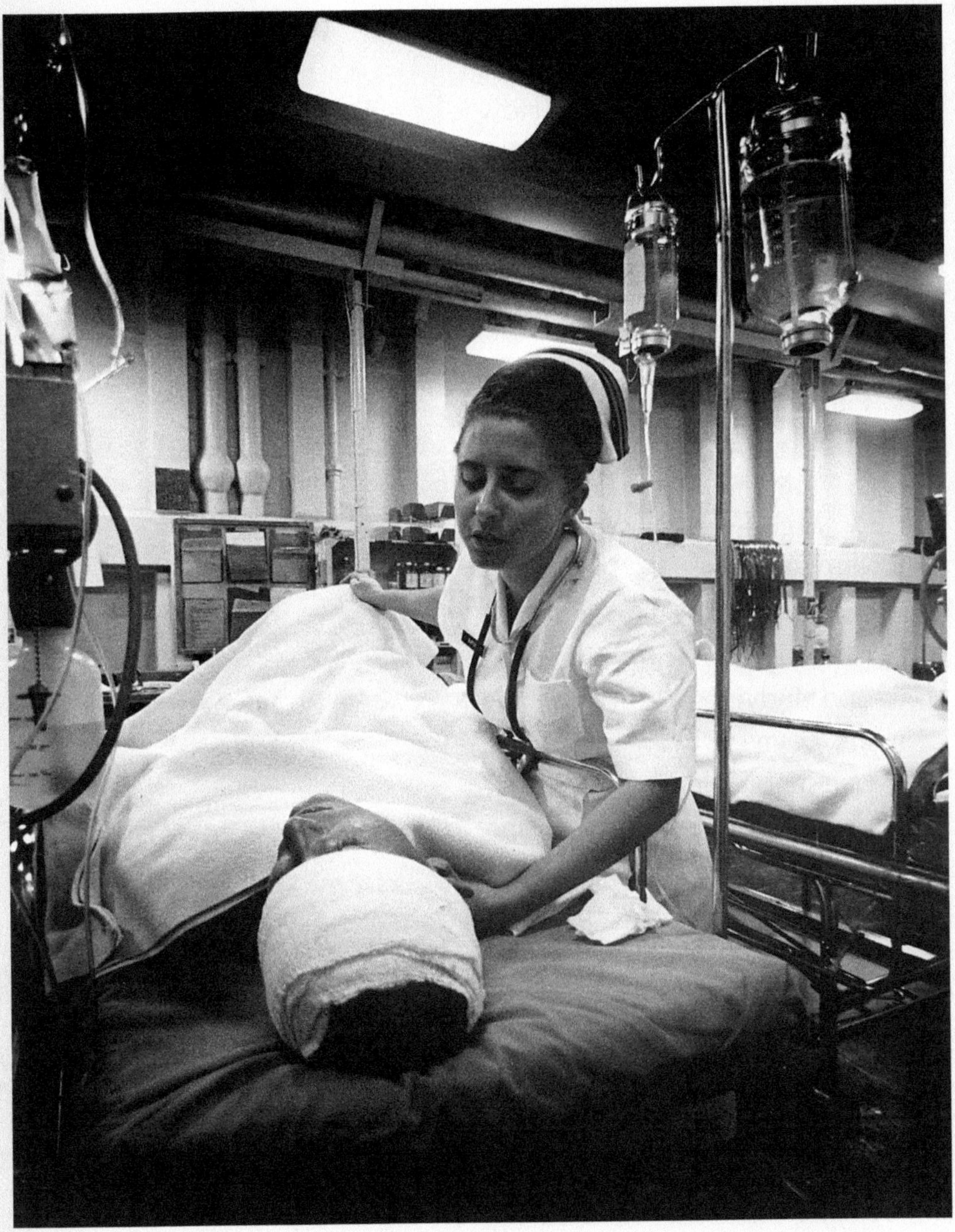

A navy nurse cares for a soldier just coming out of surgery on the USS *Repose*, a hospital ship used in the Korean War in the 1950s and in the Vietnam War.

saner, because life was pretty confusing to me when I came back," she says. "How do you make sense of a year of being where people were getting killed and maimed? I went looking for some sense and order in the world."[5] She also hoped to recapture the sense of community and purpose she had had in Vietnam.

Murphy didn't find what she was looking for at the convent. She spent the next twenty years living, working, and studying in places across the country. Eventually, after being ordained a minister in the Anglican Church, she moved to Canada, where she worked for several years as a parish priest. She went on to teach at a seminary.

PTSD and Working Toward the Future

When the Vietnam Women's Memorial was dedicated, Murphy was asked to volunteer her services as a minister. "It was the first time I'd ever really thought about my time in Vietnam," she says. "Once I started doing that,

Vietnam War veterans who served as nurses in the Sixty-Seventh Combat Support Hospital at Qui Nhon comfort each other during the dedication of the Vietnam Women's Memorial on November 11, 1993.

all hell broke loose."[6] She began to experience severe bouts of depression, anxiety attacks, and flashbacks. At the memorial, she attended a conference on PTSD and recognized that she, too, suffered from the illness. Although PTSD still affects her life, she is able to manage its symptoms with medication and self-awareness.

Although fewer Vietnam vets live in Canada, online forums and support groups have put her in contact with other women who served in Vietnam. "Sometimes I just want to forget everything, but it is helpful to know that there are people out there who I can write to and talk to, people who will understand if I'm having a rough time. Unless you've been in a war situation, it's really hard to explain it to somebody," she says.[7]

In the early 2000s, Murphy returned to Vietnam. "It's been very healing to see what the country is like without war," she says. "You'd think that they would really hate Westerners, but the people are wonderful. They say the war's over, you're our friends, and we're glad you came to see us."[8]

5

An Antiwar Servicewoman: Army Nurse Susan O'Neill

After she graduated from high school, Susan O'Neill hoped to go to college, but her parents wanted their daughter to be well-equipped for the working world and told her they would only pay for her education if she went to trade school. Given the choice between trade school and having to fund her own college education, O'Neill picked the former and decided to attend nursing school, which she expected would lead to good job opportunities.

When O'Neill's nursing school roommate decided to go to Chicago to enlist, O'Neill tagged along, happy to get a weekend out of town. She had little interest in enlisting herself—O'Neill was part of the antiwar movement, singing protest songs in coffeehouses and campaigning for antiwar politicians. The antiwar movement was widespread, and the methods people used varied widely—some protests became violent, though most were peaceful. The Vietnam War was not popular in the United States, especially among young people, and as the war went on, more and

more Americans began to believe it had been a mistake to get involved in the conflict.

But O'Neill's antiwar beliefs couldn't shake economic realities. In Chicago, a recruiter told her that if she joined the military, the government would pay for her last year of nursing school. O'Neill liked the idea of paying back her parents for her education. Still, she wasn't willing to go to Vietnam. The recruiter assured her that she wouldn't: "He said, 'You don't have to worry about Vietnam, there's a waiting list a mile long for nurses to go there.'"[1] He told her there was a good chance that she would be sent to Japan, Germany, or even Hawaii. O'Neill hadn't had many opportunities to travel; she decided the offer was too good to pass up. As she signed the necessary forms that summer of 1967, she thought about

Vietnam War protesters participate in a sing-along during a gathering in Albany, New York, in October 1969. The sign asks for the troops still serving in Vietnam to be brought home.

how surprised her friends would be that she, an antiwar protester, had enlisted.

A Death-Filled Introduction

The military exercises at basic training at Fort Sam Houston, in Texas, seemed like a waste of time to O'Neill. Why did she need to learn how to march or read a compass? Then, during one orientation, she remembers that an officer told the trainees, "You might have heard that there was a waiting list a mile long for nurses to go to Vietnam. Well, that's no longer true. By the end of this year, half of you will be there and the other half will be on orders."[2] O'Neill was stunned. In May 1969, she had orders to go to Vietnam.

The flight to Vietnam was long and quiet. Although the plane was full of servicemen and women, few wanted to discuss the war. "We avoided discussing it; it was a given," she explains.[3] On arriving in Vietnam, O'Neill was assigned to work at the Twenty-Second Surgical MUST unit (mobile hospital) in Phu Bai, located in the hills between the demilitarized zone and Da Nang. Constructed of inflated rubber hung over metal frames, MUST units could be taken apart quickly and moved as needed.

When she arrived in Phu Bai, O'Neill noticed that the countryside was covered with mounds of earth decorated with piles of white stones. Later, she learned that the US compound had been built over a Buddhist cemetery. "The tent for the motor pool actually dissected a grave," she remembers. "I was outraged. I thought what would we do if somebody set up in one of our graveyards?"[4]

Shortly after her arrival, she witnessed her first operating room death. After this initiation, she felt her work in Vietnam had truly begun. Because patients required medical attention on several injuries at once, nurses were asked to perform procedures that they were not normally expected—or even permitted—to do back in the United States. Among other things, nurses started IVs, picked shrapnel out of wounds, cut away dead tissue, and clipped damaged blood vessels.

Woman in a Man's World

On the rare occasions that she had free time, O'Neill socialized with the enlisted men who worked around her. The experience of being a woman amid hundreds of men

Medical Advances in the Vietnam War

War has always been a major catalyst for invention, especially when it comes to weaponry and medicine. Many antibiotics, for instance, were either discovered or put into widespread use during World War II. Some of the biggest medical advances during the Vietnam War had to do with emergency medicine and access to care. The Vietnam War saw the introduction of helicopter evacuations and what we know of as emergency medical care—for the first time, paramedics were trained to provide emergency services before bringing the wounded to hospitals. Severe, life-threatening situations could be treated on the ground. Soldiers who might have otherwise died from their injuries were now given lifesaving care before being evacuated, increasing the chances that they would live long enough to get thorough treatment back at the hospital. During the war, major advances were also made in the use of blood transfusions.

was strange. "People looked at you symbolically more than anything," she explains. "You were the woman they couldn't have, because sheer numbers said they couldn't. You were pressured for a lot of things. There were a number of women who I've talked to who were raped over there. I was very lucky. There was an attempt; luckily, I managed to foil it."[5]

Women in Vietnam were subject to various forms of sexual harassment and rape. Because the crimes were rarely reported, it is difficult to find statistics on these incidents. One reason for this is that the military—mirroring society at large—did not take such crimes seriously at that time. Often, women themselves were blamed for having provoked the attacks. Some women worried that reporting a colleague or superior might brand them as troublemakers and do harm to their careers. Some feared that admitting that they had been the victim of a sexual assault would demonstrate that they were unable to protect themselves and therefore weaker than their male counterparts. For these and other reasons, sexual harassment has continued to be a problem in the military.

From Phu Bai to Chu Lai to Cu Chi

By July 1969, the United States was beginning its plan to "Vietnamize" the war—that is, turn over the responsibility of fighting the North Vietnamese army to the South Vietnamese government. The number of US troops stationed in Vietnam was scaled back. Two months after O'Neill's arrival in Phu Bai, the MUST unit was packed up and its staff dispersed to other hospitals. O'Neill was sent to work at the Twenty-Seventh Surgical at Chu Lai. The hospital was

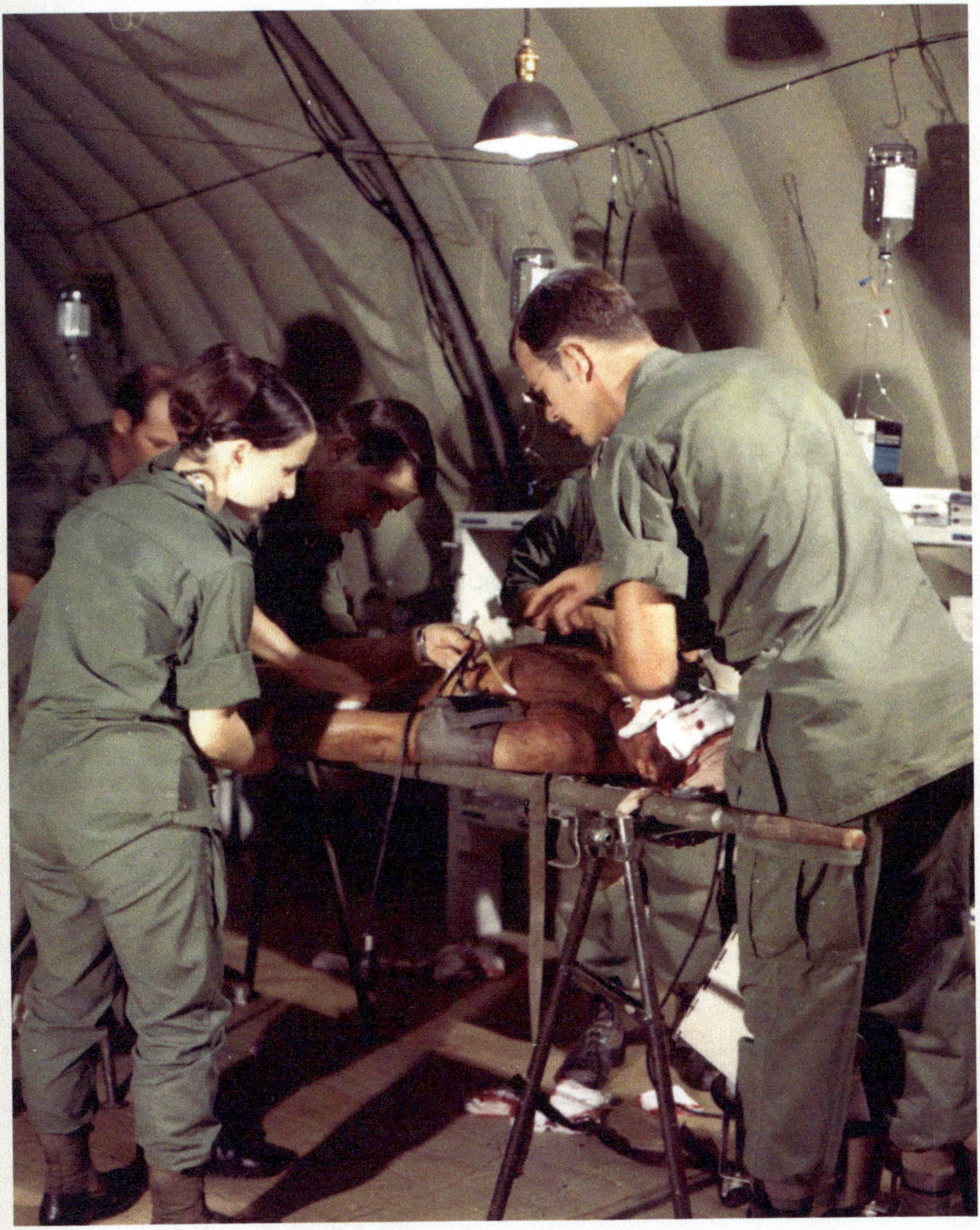

Corporal Bernice Scott (*left*) of the Army Nurse Corps works with a medical team to treat a patient at the Second Surgical Hospital in Lai Khe in 1969.

one of two on a sprawling military complex situated south of Phu Bai, on the coast of the South China Sea.

The small, overworked staff at the Twenty-Second MUST unit in Phu Bai had had little time to follow the demands of military protocol. The hospital at Chu Lai, however, was far less busy. Also, a number of "lifers," or people intending to make a career out of their military service, were based in Chu Lai. The hospital was far more concerned about proper military conduct. Dress codes, obligatory saluting, and rules of fraternization—officers were not allowed to socialize with enlisted men or women—were strictly enforced. O'Neill didn't care for such rules. She was often in trouble with the hospital's head nurse. O'Neill requested a transfer. The head nurse told her she would transfer her into one of the heaviest combat zones in Vietnam—the Twelfth Evacuation Hospital in Cu Chi.

Cu Chi was a key location during the war. Between 1945 and 1975, more than 75 miles (121 km) of multilevel underground tunnels and chambers were carved beneath Saigon and the surrounding Cu Chi province. Built during France's occupation, the tunnels were expanded during the Vietnam War. The intricate network housed an entire community. It included meeting rooms, kitchens, sleeping quarters, schools, and hospitals. The Vietcong used the tunnels to plan and execute attacks against US and South Vietnamese forces.

Thousands of Vietnamese civilians took shelter in the tunnels during US bombings, and US forces made several attempts to clear the tunnels. Cu Chi became one of the most heavily bombed and defoliated sites in Vietnam. Despite these efforts, the tunnels remained largely intact for the duration of the war. The tunnels have come to symbolize the endurance and ingenuity of the Vietnamese people. Today, the tunnels' entrances have been widened to accommodate curious tourists.

Although O'Neill's assignment at Cu Chi was supposed to be a punishment, O'Neill was glad to be in Cu Chi. "I wanted to go some place that was relatively busy," she says. "You have to think too much if you have a lot of spare time. I was asking myself entirely too many questions and getting pretty depressed. 'Why am I here? What good am I doing? If I'm opposed to this war, am I morally bound to leave?'"[6] As long as she was busy helping patients, she felt useful and could justify being in Vietnam.

"Your Country Is Proud"

O'Neill counted the days until her return to the United States. At the same time, she wondered how she would fit in. She had kept in touch with her family by trading recorded tapes, but she rarely talked about the war. She didn't want them to worry. Once, though, toward the end of her assignment, she sat outside when she was making her tape, so the sounds of artillery shelling could be heard. "I wanted them to think in terms of the war, because they believed most anything the government said. I was pretty bitter at that point. I wanted them to get the atmosphere of it and realize that there was something going on over here," she remembers.[7]

Twenty-four hours after O'Neill left Vietnam, she arrived at a military base in Oakland, California. She remembers walking down a long corridor that seemed to go on forever. "At the end of it, there was a mural of a soldier standing there with a flag," she says. "Underneath was written, 'Welcome Back Soldier—Your Country is Proud of You.'"

Military medical personnel treated civilians as well as soldiers. Here, Lieutenant Mary Huepers, an army nurse, opens a bottle of alcohol to treat a young patient.

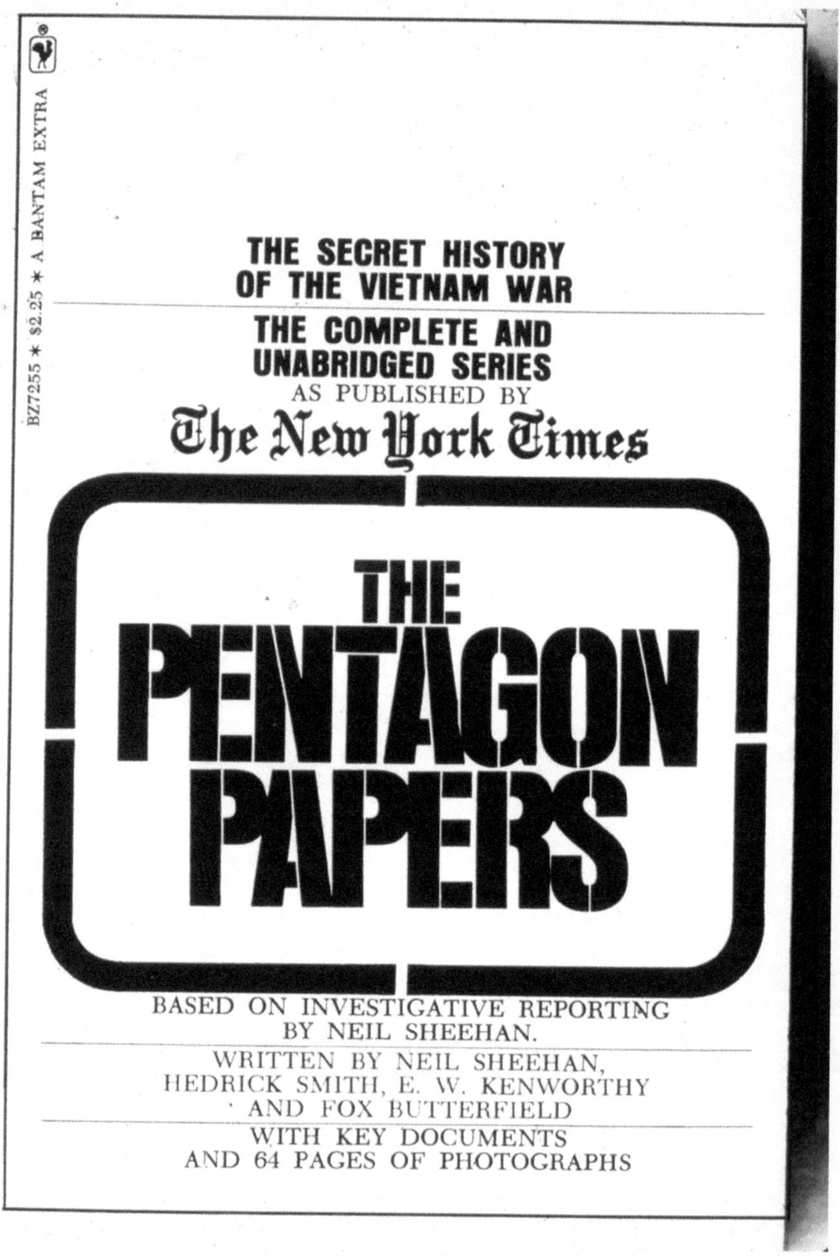

The Pentagon Papers were released to the public by the *New York Times* and revealed that the government had been misleading the public about American involvement in Vietnam for years.

O'Neill knew this wasn't true. Most Americans were not proud of Vietnam vets; many were ashamed. They felt that vets had killed innocent civilians and destroyed villages for no reason. "We followed the news," she said. "You could get the *New York Times* and *Time* magazine, so you knew what was going on."[8]

Rather than return to Indiana, O'Neill decided to stay in Oakland. There she met with a boyfriend, the hospital registrar with whom she had worked in Cu Chi. He asked her to marry him, and O'Neill accepted. Because she had a companion who understood and shared so many of her experiences in Vietnam, O'Neill believes that the relationship saved her from experiencing some of the psychological problems that other, more isolated vets faced.

Twenty-five years after O'Neill returned from Vietnam, she began writing about her experiences there. Ballantine Books published a collection of these stories, *Don't Mean Nothing*, in 2001. In her introduction to the collection, O'Neill writes: "I joined the army for the money and the travel, and because I was naive and had no idea what I would be getting myself into. It was one of the biggest learning experiences of my life."[9]

6

Triage and Trauma: Army Nurse Diana Sebek

Diana Sebek wanted to become an army nurse from an early age, but her idea of war was nothing like the real thing. As a young girl, Sebek became entranced by the romanticized images of World War II nurses she saw in books and movies. "There was a John Wayne movie showing nuns walking into battle to deliver care to the wounded soldiers," she recalls. "They just walked right through the gunfire and were so powerful, they weren't hurt. In my six-year-old mind, I thought that was marvelous."[1]

Sebek also associated World War II nurses with her aunt, who had been a nurse and whom Sebek greatly admired. Being a nurse seemed both noble and adventuresome, and Sebek eventually enrolled in a nursing school program at the South Chicago Community Hospital after graduating from high school. Tragically, while Sebek was a student, nine of her classmates were raped and murdered by a man who was later arrested. It's possible that this terrifying event led to Sebek's enlistment, as the army would allow Sebek to leave Chicago and offered her a sense of security. Sebek was introduced to the army student nursing program by a roommate, and when army recruiters offered to pay one year of tuition in exchange for two years of active military service, Sebek joined without a second thought.

Entering the Unknown

Busy in nursing school, Sebek was largely sheltered from news about the war. On the rare occasions when Sebek had free time, watching television was the last thing she wanted to do. Consequently, she had little idea what she might be facing. "The thought of going to war was not even in my head," she says. "Basically, I thought I could pay my parents back for school. And then when I was in the service, I wouldn't have to worry about a place to live; it was kind of like marrying Uncle Sam."[2]

After Sebek graduated and passed her state board exams, she was officially on duty. Her first

John Wayne hugs a young nurse, played by Anna Lee, in this still from the film *Flying Tigers*, a propaganda film about World War II released in 1942.

requirement was to report to Fort Sam Houston for basic training. She sat in an auditorium with other nurses and doctors, where they learned about military insignia and protocol or, as she puts it, "who you were expected to salute, who was expected to salute you."[3] She also learned to march in formation. "I hated marching," she says. "It was like being in a meat market, like cattle being moved around. The guys on the side would whistle and make noises."[4] More useful was the additional medical combat training, including learning how to perform tracheotomies (making air passages in the throat by cutting a hole in the trachea).

At the time of her training, Sebek was engaged to an antiwar activist. He wanted to get her pregnant in order to release her from her military service. But during basic training, Sebek felt herself beginning to change. She realized there were more opportunities open to her other than marriage and motherhood. She broke up with her fiancé. "And then the world was in front of me," she remembers. "I was joining the army, not thinking or worrying about war or people getting killed."[5]

On December 5, 1969, Sebek was at the airport, waiting to fly to Vietnam. Her family all came to see her off. During the picture taking and farewells, she was scared, but excited: "I was the man in the 1962 movie *Hemingway's Adventures of a Young Man*," she recalls. "I was a young woman, but I was going to have the same adventures as a man."[6]

The twenty-four-hour flight to Vietnam was long and tiring. Aside from the flight attendants, Sebek was the only woman aboard the plane. Not that this bothered her: "I talked to the guys. To me, there was no difference between me and them. We were army; we were going over, fine. It's amazing how naive I was."[7]

Who Lives and Dies

She landed at an airport in Cam Ranh Bay, where she was struck by the smell of burning garbage and bodies. Here she had to wait for another flight to take her up north to her destination, Quang Tri, to a hospital close to the demilitarized zone. It was a marine hospital connected to a Vietnamese children's hospital. Many of the wounded were army and air force service men and Vietnamese children caught in the crossfire of battle. Originally assigned to work in an operating room, Sebek worked where she was most needed—in triage.

It was extremely difficult for Sebek to talk about what she saw and did that year. Every day, she was faced with critically wounded and dying men. She cleaned their wounds and sent them to the operating room, where they were put under anesthesia. She never got a chance to talk to them or connect their faces with names. Some of the friends she made in Vietnam were killed. She became severely depressed and had trouble coming to terms with what she was seeing and doing in Vietnam. A doctor prescribed antidepressants and sent her to a hospital in Da Nang to see a psychiatrist.

As it turns out, the psychiatrist Sebek was assigned to see was not working at the hospital but was a patient in the hospital. While she waited for him to see her, she saw the movie *M*A*S*H*, a dark comedy about US military doctors and nurses in the Korean War. The movie helped Sebek realize that her depression and feelings of futility over the war were normal. "It gave some validation to the fact that the war was a farce," she says.[8] When she heard that her unit was receiving mass casualties, she returned to work without having seen the psychiatrist.

The Horrors of Returning Home

When her tour of duty was over, Sebek was ready to go home. The return was more difficult than she had imagined.

Like Vietnam War nurses, World War II nurses had to train for life in the jungle. In this 1947 image, army nurses, led by Lieutenant Olive V. Grenier, train for their deployment on the India-Burma border.

"I did not realize that people were calling Vietnam veterans 'baby-killers,' that there were actually people who hated us."[9] When she told people that she had served in Vietnam, people turned away from her. "It was personal," she says. "I thought I was unlovable. I thought it was Diana, not the fact that I was a Vietnam veteran."[10]

She began to suffer from post-traumatic stress disorder. She found it impossible to talk to anyone and wanted to be alone. Her family reacted to her growing isolation with anger and confusion: "My mother told me that the army 'messed' me up, only that wasn't the word she used. I had to move out of the house because I couldn't handle being told that I was so 'messed' up."[11]

She took a job at a veterans hospital. Because the patients had been in wars themselves, Sebek felt accepted. She tried to contact a few of the people she'd known in Vietnam, but survivor's guilt eventually made her afraid to keep in touch. Were her friends still alive? Would they be missing a leg or arm?

FAZKX
U.S.A

US Army nurses Captain Gladys Sepulveda and Second Lieutenant Lois Ferrari await transportation to the Eighth Field Hospital at Nha Trang in July 1965.

Treatment in Triage

Triage is the process of assigning different degrees of priority to different patients and deciding who needs the most urgent care. It's seen most often in situations where there are mass casualties, like major accidents or in wartime. The triage unit has the difficult job of choosing which patients need help immediately, which patients can wait a little longer for care, and which patients are just too wounded to be helped. In the triage unit, nurses and corpsmen (military field medics) separated the wounded according to who needed to be seen first. Sometimes, if a soldier was likely to die, the medical staff had to move on to treat those men who had a chance of living. Determining which patients would die and which might live was traumatic. Many triage nurses were burdened by guilt and questioned their decisions for the rest of their lives.

Rather than risk learning more tragic news, she avoided her past experiences as much as possible.

Over the next thirty years, Sebek struggled with PTSD. Eventually, she began experiencing severe flashbacks at work and was forced to retire. She went to therapy to try to cope with the symptoms of PTSD. Part of her therapy was to remember and talk about what she experienced in Vietnam. The memories create physical and emotional pain. "People were sent to just kill," she says. "It was disgusting, animal against animal. I have so many empty spaces in my head about things that occurred there. I don't know what memories are there. Going back is hard."[12]

Sebek found comfort in the movie *M*A*S*H*, which followed doctors in the Korean War and led to a long-running television show of the same name, a still from which can be seen here.

Like Sebek, most women who served in Vietnam, no matter their job title, suffered trauma. They witnessed death, destruction, and maiming. Because they were women, they were expected to provide comfort and cheer even when they themselves felt none. They held men's hands as they were dying and became surrogate mothers, wives, and girlfriends to men whose loved ones were far away. They tended the needs of others, with little time or energy left over to care for themselves.

Chronology

939 The Chinese are driven out of Vietnam. The era of Vietnamese independence begins.

1884 The French colonial era begins.

1930 Ho Chi Minh establishes Indochinese Communist Party and organizes campaign to win Vietnamese independence.

1940 Japan places Vietnam under military occupation. Local French authority is weakened to figurehead status.

1945 The Japanese surrender to the Allies, ending World War II. Vietnamese Communist Party under Ho Chi Minh declares Vietnam's independence as the Democratic Republic of Vietnam (DRV). French troops return to Vietnam.

1950 The United States begins to give economic and military aid to French troops in Vietnam.

1954 French troops are defeated. Geneva Accords divide Vietnam at the 17th Parallel. North Vietnam is independent under a socialist government. South Vietnam is governed as a republic under President Ngo Dinh Diem, with US support. Elections to unite the two regions under one government are to be held in two years.

1955 President Diem announces elections won't take place. The United States begins sending money and military advisers to South Vietnam.

1956 Vietnamese communists push President Diem for elections. Diem cracks down on political opponents.

1959 North Vietnam sends weapons and supplies to the Vietcong on the Ho Chi Minh Trail.

1960 Newly elected US president John F. Kennedy promises to help South Vietnam.

1961 The United States starts to use chemical warfare and sprays forests in Vietnam with Agent Orange in order to expose Vietcong fighters. USAID is established by the executive order of President John F. Kennedy.

1963 President Diem is killed in a military coup. More than 16,300 US military personnel are stationed in Vietnam. US president John F. Kennedy dies.

1964 Lyndon B. Johnson wins the US presidential election. US Congress passes the Gulf of Tonkin Resolution, giving President Johnson authority to take military action against North Vietnam in response to an alleged North Vietnamese attack on the USS *Maddox*, a US Navy destroyer that had been in the gulf, spying on North Vietnam. During his presidency, Johnson uses the resolution to justify sending increasing numbers of troops to fight in Vietnam.

1965 The first US combat troops, army and navy nurses, and civilian volunteers arrive in Vietnam.

1967 President Johnson allows women to achieve general and admiral rank.

1968 The Tet Offensive by the North Vietnamese army and its sympathizers is waged against targets in South Vietnam on January 31. Richard M. Nixon is elected US president.

1969 Ho Chi Minh dies on September 3. The United States begins plan to "Vietnamize" the war. More than sixty thousand American soldiers are withdrawn from Vietnam.

1970 The United States and North Vietnam begin secret negotiations to end war. The US National Guard opens fire on students during antiwar rally at Kent State University, killing four students and injuring nine others.

1971 The *New York Times* publishes the Pentagon Papers, classified government documents leaked to the press indicating that the US government had been intentionally dishonest to the public about its involvement in Vietnam.

1972 On March 29, the last contingent of American nurses leaves Vietnam. More than five thousand nurses served during the war; the average age was 23.6 years old. On August 11, the last US combat troops withdraw from Vietnam. Nixon is reelected.

1973 The United States and North Vietnam sign a cease-fire agreement in Paris on January 27. US ground troops withdraw from Vietnam.

1975 The South Vietnamese army retreats under a North Vietnamese offensive. The last Americans are evacuated on April 29. North Vietnamese troops enter Saigon on April 30. Congress orders three military academies to accept female cadets.

1976 North and South Vietnam are united as the Socialist Republic of Vietnam.

1977 The Socialist Republic of Vietnam is admitted to the United Nations.

1982 The Vietnam Veterans Memorial is dedicated in Washington, DC, on November 11.

1984 The Vietnam Women's Memorial Project is established.

1993 The Vietnam Women's Memorial is dedicated in Washington, DC, on November 11.

1994 The United States ends its embargo on Vietnam.

1997 Full diplomatic relations and the exchange of ambassadors are established between the United States and Vietnam. The Women in Military Service for America Memorial opens at Arlington National Cemetery.

2013 The Obama administration announces an end to the ban on women in combat.

Chapter Notes

Chapter 1

Treatment for All: Army Nurse Kathy Fennel

1. Kathy Fennel, telephone interview, April 20, 2003.
2. Fennel.
3. Fennel.
4. Fennel.
5. Fennel.
6. Fennel.

Chapter 2

Building and Rebuilding: USAID Administrator Barbara Rozell

1. Barbara Rozell, telephone interview, April 12, 2003.
2. Karen Zeinhert, *The Valiant Women of the Vietnam War* (Brookfield, CT: The Millbrook Press, 2000), p. 40.
3. Rozell.
4. Rozell.
5. Rozell.
6. Rozell.
7. Rozell.
8. Rozell.
9. Rozell.
10. Rozell.

Chapter 3

Healing in a War Zone: Army Nurse Diane Carlson Evans

1. Diane Carlson Evans, telephone interview, April 20, 2003.
2. Evans.

3. Evans.
4. Evans.
5. Evans.
6. Evans.
7. Evans.
8. Evans.
9. Diane Carlson Evans, "Moving a Vision: The Vietnam Women's Memorial," http://www.vietnamwomensmemorial.org/pdf/dcevans.pdf (accessed May 15, 2019).

Chapter 4

A Hospital at Sea: Navy Nurse Beth Marie Murphy

1. Beth Marie Murphy, telephone interview, April 18, 2003.
2. Murphy.
3. Murphy.
4. Murphy.
5. Murphy.
6. Murphy.
7. Murphy.
8. Murphy.

Chapter 5

An Antiwar Servicewoman: Army Nurse Susan O'Neill

1. Susan O'Neill, telephone interview, April 12, 2003.
2. O'Neill.
3. O'Neill.
4. O'Neill.
5. O'Neill.
6. O'Neill.
7. O'Neill.

8. O'Neill.
9. Susan O'Neill, *Don't Mean Nothing: Short Stories of Vietnam* (New York: Ballantine Books, 2001), xii.

Chapter 6

Triage and Trauma: Army Nurse Diana Sebek

1. Diana Sebek, telephone interview, April 17, 2003.
2. Sebek.
3. Sebek.
4. Sebek.
5. Sebek.
6. Sebek.
7. Sebek.
8. Sebek.
9. Sebek.
10. Sebek.
11. Sebek.
12. Sebek.

Glossary

communist One in favor of establishing a communist political system, similar to the Communist Party system established in Russia in 1917. In theory, under communism, society's economic and social needs are determined and met by the state, rather than by a free-market economy or social class.

fraternization Association with others in a friendly, brotherly way, usually in violation of rules or orders that prohibit such interactions.

Ho Chi Minh Trail A maze of footpaths and roads used by the North Vietnamese army and Vietcong soldiers to ship supplies from North Vietnam to South Vietnam.

hooch A general term for hutlike living quarters used to house military personnel in base camps; also used to refer to the thatch and bamboo homes of the rural Vietnamese.

medevac A portmanteau of "medical evacuation"; the transportation of injured individuals to a hospital, usually by helicopter.

monsoon A seasonal wind in South and Southeast Asia, or the rains brought by the wet monsoon from May to September.

MUST unit Acronym for medical unit self-transportable; a hospital constructed in such a way that it can be moved easily from one area to another.

North Vietnam As part of the 1954 negotiations for France's withdrawal from Vietnam, France and North Vietnam agreed to divide Vietnam at the 17th Parallel, between the predominately communist northern part of the country and the retreating French and their Vietnamese supporters in the southern part.

post-traumatic stress disorder (PTSD) A psychological disorder caused by experiencing an extremely traumatic event; symptoms include flashbacks, amnesia, depression, and uncontrollable emotional and physical reactions to stimuli.

prisoner of war (POW) A soldier who has been captured by the opposing military forces.

South Vietnam After Vietnam was divided at the 17th Parallel, South Vietnam was ruled by President Ngo Dinh Diem. In order to keep South Vietnam from a North Vietnamese communist takeover, US president Johnson approved a US military offensive against North Vietnam.

Tet Offensive A major military campaign against cities and towns throughout South Vietnam led by the communist forces in North and South Vietnam on Tet, the Vietnamese New Year.

transfusion The process of transferring blood from one person to another, used in situations where the injured person has lost so much blood that he or she is in danger of going into shock and dying.

triage The process of assigning priority to multiple patients, usually used in situations where there are mass casualties, like accidents and wartime.

Vietcong (VC) Refers to Vietnamese communists and their supporters who fought against South Vietnamese and US troops during the Vietnam War; taken from the Vietnamese equivalent for "Vietnamese Communist," Vietnam Cong-san.

Vietnam Veterans Memorial Commonly referred to as the Wall, the memorial in Washington, DC, is a black, granite wall built in 1982 and dedicated to US servicemen and women who died or went missing during their tours of duty in Vietnam. The polished stone is carved with more than fifty-eight thousand names. In 1993, the Vietnam Women's Memorial, a sculpture depicting three nurses tending to a wounded soldier, was added to honor women who served in the war.

Women's Army Corps (WAC) An auxiliary noncombat army unit established for female volunteers by the US Congress in 1942. By the end of World War II, more than ninety-nine thousand women had served in the WAC, both overseas and in the United States. In 1948, Congress passed the Women's Armed Services Integration Act, and the WAC became part of the regular army.

Bibliography

Bigler, Philip. *Hostile Fire: The Life and Death of First Lieutenant Sharon Lane*. Arlington, VA: Vandamere Press, 1996.

Bunn, Austin. "Unarmed and Under Fire: An Oral History of Female Vietnam Vets." Salon.com, November 11, 1999. www.salon.com/1999/11/11/women_4/.

Diagnostic and Statistical Manual of Mental Disorders, 3rd ed. Washington, DC: American Psychiatric Association, 1987.

Evans, Diane Carlson. "Moving a Vision: The Vietnam Women's Memorial." Accessed May 3, 2019. www.vietnamwomensmemorial.org/pdf/dcevans.pdf.

Evans, Diane Carlson. Telephone interview. April 17, 2003.

Fennel, Kathy. Telephone interview. April 20, 2003.

Fenner, Lorry M., and Marie E. de Young. *Women in Combat: Civic Duty or Military Liability?* Washington, DC: Georgetown University Press, 2001.

Gruhzit-Hoyt, Olga. *A Time Remembered: American Women in the Vietnam War*. Novato, CA: Presidio Press, 1999.

Koehn, Donna. "Military Museum of Their Own," *Tampa Tribune*, April 4, 2001, p. 1.

Mason, Patience. Telephone interview. April 14, 2003.

Murphy, Beth Marie. Telephone interview. April 18, 2003.

No Time for Tears: Vietnam: The Women Who Served. Videocassette. West End Films, Inc., 1993.

Olson, James, and Rancy Roberts. *My Lai: A Brief History with Documents.* Boston: Bedford Books, 1998.

O'Neill, Susan. Telephone interview. April 12, 2003.

"Portfolio: Warrior Women." *New York Times Magazine,* February 16, 2003.

Rozell, Barbara. Telephone interview. April 12, 2003.

Scheider, Pat. "Women Veterans Sought for Benefits" *Capital Times,* November 10, 2001, p. 2.

Sebek, Diana. Telephone interview. April 16, 2003.

Skaine, Rosemarie. *Women at War: Gender Issues of Americans in Combat.* Jefferson, NC: McFarland & Co., 1999.

Steinman, Ron. *Inside Television's First War: A Saigon Journal.* Columbia, MO: University of Missouri Press, 2002.

Stur, Heather Marie. *Beyond Combat: Women and Gender in the Vietnam War Era.* New York: Cambridge University Press, 2011.

Templer, Robert. *Shadows and Wind: A View of Modern Vietnam.* New York: Penguin Books, 1999.

Turner, Karen Gottschang, and Phan Thanh Hao. *Even the Women Must Fight: Memories of War from North Vietnam.* New York: John Wiley & Sons, 1998.

Ward, Geoffrey C., and Ken Burns. *The Vietnam War: An Intimate History.* New York: Knopf, 2017.

Zeinert, Karen. *The Valiant Women of the Vietnam War.* Brookfield, CT: Millbrook Press, 2000.

Further Reading

Books

DeCarlo, Carolyn. *Great Exit Projects on the Vietnam War and the Antiwar Movement.* New York, NY: Rosen Central, 2019.

Neville, Peter. *Ho Chi Minh*. New York, NY: Routledge, 2018.

Simons, Lisa. *Women in Combat: Bringing the Fight to the Front Lines.* North Mankato, MN: Capstone Press, 2017.

Staats, Ann McCallum. *Women Heroes of the US Army: Remarkable Soldiers from the American Revolution to Today*. Chicago, IL: Chicago Review Press, 2019.

Tinari, Leah. *The Presidents: Portraits of History*. New York, NY: Aladdin, 2019.

Tougas, Shelley. *Weapons, Gear, and Uniforms of the Vietnam War.* North Mankato, MN: Capstone Press, 2018.

Websites

National Women's History Museum

https://www.womenshistory.org

The website for the National Women's History Museum in Alexandria, Virginia, offers digitized exhibits, articles, and other resources about women throughout American history.

US Army Women's Museum

https://awm.lee.army.mil

The United States Army Women's Museum is located in Fort Lee, Virginia, and its website offers a guide to its exhibits and useful articles about women throughout army history.

The Vietnam Veterans Memorial

http://thewall-usa.com

The Vietnam Veterans Memorial website allows users to search names on the Wall, view images related to the war, and explore information about the war and the memorial.

Index

H

J

K

L

M

N

O

P

Q